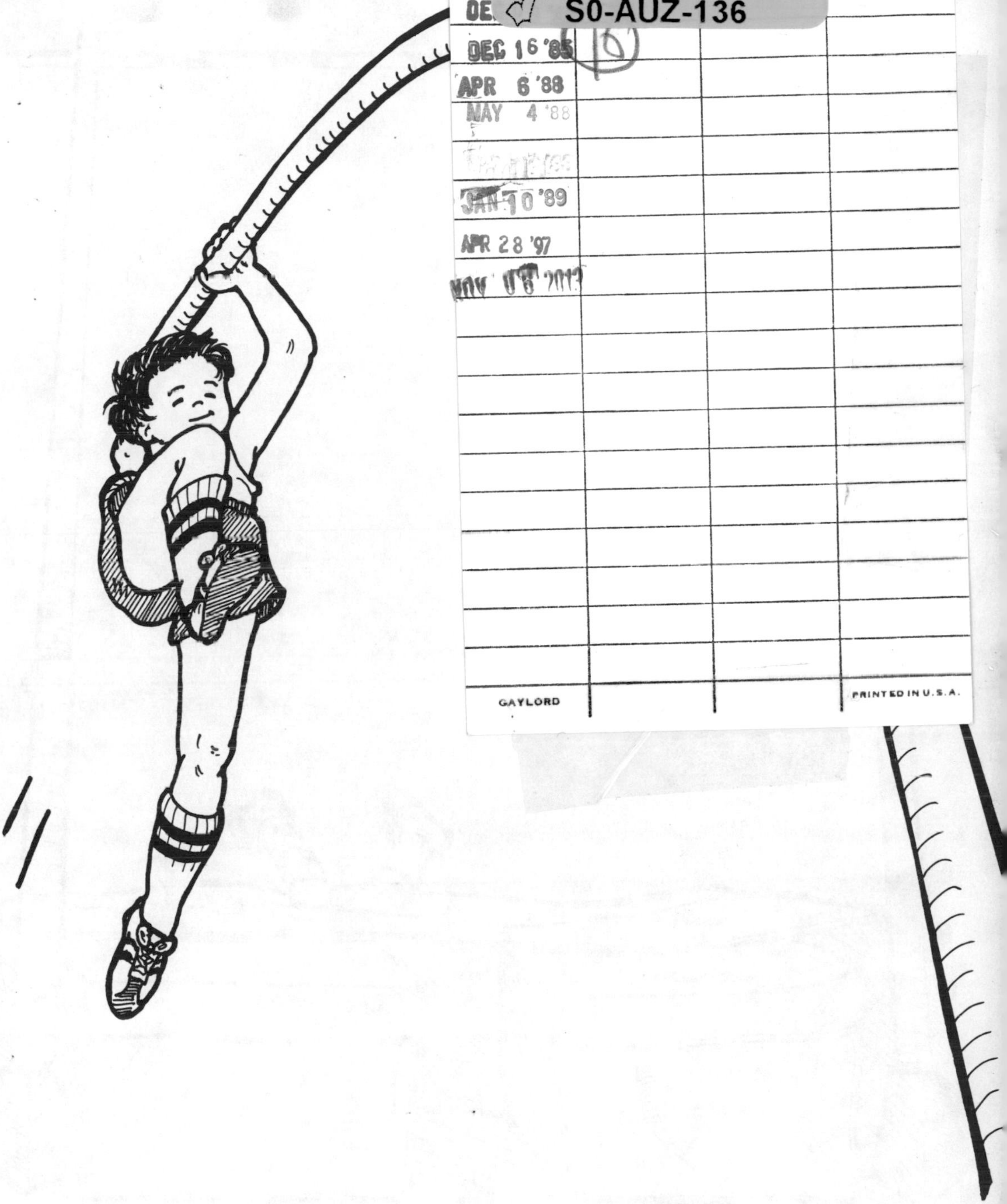

ILLUSTRATED TRACK AND FIELD DICTIONARY FOR YOUNG PEOPLE

BY PHYLLIS RAYBIN EMERT

ILLUSTRATED BY

MARIETTA FOSTER SMITH

PRENTICE-HALL, INC.
Englewood Cliffs, New Jersey

Track is the sport of the Gods. It is one sport where the opponent is never hurt physically. A track man tires his competitor, dares him, matches him in his challenge for victory, but never harasses him. Author Unknown

For Mother and Dad

The author gratefully acknowledges the assistance and cooperation of Vincent Reel, Editor of *Women's Track World Magazine,* Pete Cava, Press Information Director of The Athletics Congress of the USA, Irene Mazura, Reference Librarian and most particularly, Larry Emert.

Illustrated Track and Field Dictionary for Young People
Copyright © 1981
by Harvey House, Publishers

Treehouse Paperback edition published 1981 by Prentice-Hall Inc. by arrangement with Harvey House, Publishers

Printed in the United States of America • J
10 9 8 7 6 5 4 3 2 1

Library of Congress Cataloging in Publication Data
Emert, Phyllis Raybin.
Illustrated track and field dictionary for young people.
Summary: An illustrated guide to track and field events.
1. Track-athletics—Dictionaries, Juvenile.
[1. Track and field—Dictionaries]   I. Smith, Marietta Foster.   II. Title.
GV1060.5.E46   1981   796.4'2'03   81-1532
ISBN 0-13-451310-X (pbk.)   AACR2

FOREWORD

Many have called track and field the oldest sport in the world. In prehistoric times, wild animals wandered the earth freely. Man quickly learned to run fast and jump far to escape these savage beasts. To survive he found out how to hunt smaller animals for food by throwing sharpened sticks or heavy rocks. Those who lived the longest could run faster, jump farther and throw longer and harder than their enemies.

In ancient Greece these skills were still important for survival. There were many wars and soldiers were admired for their physical fitness and courage. The people respected the warriors and depended on them for protection.

The Greeks held festivals where men matched their strength, speed and stamina against each other in running, jumping, wrestling and throwing contests. The top performers usually turned out to be the best soldiers. The men who competed in these games and contests were called athletes. The best athletes in Greece were great heroes to the people.

In 776 B.C. one large sports festival was held throughout the country. It was called the Olympic Games because it took place on the plain of Olympia. There was only one event, a foot race of 200 yards (one length of the field). A runner named Coroebus won the race and it became the earliest recorded track event in history.

The Games were such a great success that they were held every four years. They became so important to the Greeks that wars were stopped so athletes could take part.

As time passed new contests were added, mainly track and field events: a foot race of 400 yards (two lengths of the field), discus throwing, spear throwing, long jumping, boxing, wrestling and chariot races.

At first women weren't allowed to compete in or even watch the Games. The penalty for just attending was to be thrown off a mountain. It wasn't until the 128th Olympic Games that women were finally able to take part. Belisiche of Macedonia won the race for chariots drawn by pairs of colts.

The Games lasted for nearly 1,200 years until Emperor Theodosius I of Rome stopped them in 394 A.D.

Track and field was introduced in England in the 1100's but didn't gain real popularity until the 1800's. The first college track meet was in England in 1864 between Oxford and Cambridge. In 1866 the English held their first championship meet. Other countries took notice of the sport and started track and field programs of their own.

The New York Athletic Club sponsored the first track meet in America in 1868. It was an indoor meet and the first time that athletes wore special spiked shoes while competing. In 1871 the New York Athletic Club built the first outdoor cinder track. Interest in the sport quickly grew and the first college track meet was held in Saratoga, New York in 1874.

The Amateur Athletic Union (AAU) was formed in 1888 and became the main organization in charge of track and field in the United States. Rules and regulations were written and the AAU sponsored indoor and outdoor national championship meets each year.

There was talk throughout the world of bringing back the Olympic Games. One man worked for many years to revive the Games of ancient Greece. His name was Baron Pierre de Coubertin of France. De Coubertin believed that athletic competition among countries would lead to peace, friendship and understanding throughout the world.

In 1896, after years of planning, the first modern Olympic Games were held in Athens, Greece. There were six track and six field events on the program. Americans won nine of the 12 contests. James Connolly was the first American to ever win an Olympic championship.

Women didn't compete at the 1896 Games. They took part in swimming in 1912 and many other events in the years that followed. By 1928 women were also participating in track and field events alongside the men.

Today track and field is the main focus of the Olympic Games. More athletes compete in these events than any other. Olympic winners in track are considered by many to be the unofficial champions of the world.

Since the revival of the Olympics the sport has continued to grow throughout the world. In 1913 the International Amateur Athletic Federation (IAAF) was formed. The IAAF is in charge of all international track and field meets and decides all world records. Nearly every country in the world is a member.

Over the last 60 years there has been a steady improvement in track and field performances. Times, heights and distances which were once thought impossible are now commonplace.

In the United States the National Collegiate Athletic Association (NCAA) held its first national championship meet in 1921. The 440 yard dash (quarter mile) was won in a time of 49 seconds. Today that speed is bettered by many teenage athletes.

In 1896 William Hoyt of the United States pole vaulted 10 feet 9¾ inches to win a first place medal at the Olympic Games in Greece. At the 1980 Olympics in Moscow, Wladyslaw Kozakiewicz of Poland vaulted 18 feet 11½ inches to set a new world and Olympic record. Barriers continue to fall as runners run faster, throwers throw farther and jumpers leap longer and higher.

Today millions of men and women and boys and girls are involved in track and field activities at every level throughout the world. In the United States alone, there are thousands of track clubs and dozens of events to challenge everyone's skills.

Some events require strength and power. Others demand speed and quickness or endurance and stamina. There are events for seven-year-olds and events for 70-year-olds.

The track events include foot races of every distance, the hurdles, the steeplechase, team relay races and race walking competition. Races are run on a quarter mile (440 yard) oval track. In other parts of the world the track is 400 meters. (The difference is less than three yards.)

Most international competitions, including the Olympic Games, use the metric system which is based on the meter. Today, the mile run is the only non-metric event to be officially recognized world-wide.

The United States has also switched to the metric system, but miles, yards and inches are still used in many track and field competitions as the change-over to metric takes place. There can be a 100 yard dash and a 100 meter dash or an 880 yard run as well as an 800 meter run.

All races start with the firing of a pistol and end when the winner crosses the finish line or snaps a tape stretched across the finish line.

During the winter season, indoor meets are held. Indoor tracks are usually made of curved or flat boards and measure eight or 11 laps to the mile. The IAAF doesn't recognize world indoor records. However, The Athletics Congress of the USA (formerly the AAU) does list them.

Races run over short distances are called sprints or dashes. They're usually run at top speed from start to finish.

There are also middle distance races and long distance contests over one mile in length. Runners in these events need strength and stamina to do well.

The marathon is a race of 26 miles 385 yards. It usually starts and ends on the regular running track but is mostly run over city streets and highways. There is no recognized world record in the marathon because the courses are different from place to place.

Women run long distance events in the United States and other countries, but at the Olympic Games they have had no events longer than 1,500 meters. Beginning in 1984, a 3,000 meter race and marathon will be included for women.

Hurdles races are run over barriers 30 to 42 inches high. The height of the hurdle depends on the distance of the race and the age and sex of the competitors.

The steeplechase is a 3,000 meter race for men only. It involves jumping over 28 hurdles and seven water jumps.

12

In relay races teams of four runners compete against each other and pass a baton from runner to runner. In regular relays each competitor runs the same distance (or leg) as his teammate. In medley relays each runner covers a different distance from his teammate. In shuttle relays the runners race back and forth, one at a time, in two different directions, sometimes over hurdles.

In race walking events, competitors must always keep both feet in constant contact with the ground. Race walkers compete in events of one or two miles in length up to 50 kilometers (31 miles).

The field events in track and field competition are made up of jumping and throwing contests. These events are held on the track infield, often several at a time.

The long jump and men's triple jump are jumps for distance from a running start. The high jump and pole vault are jumps for height over a crossbar also from running starts. In the pole vault, an event for men only, the competitor uses the pole to vault over the bar. All jumpers land in pits filled with foam rubber or other soft material to cushion the force of the landing.

In the throwing events objects are thrown or hurled for distance. The shot put, javelin and discus are throwing events for both men and women. The hammer and heavy weight throws (35 pounds and 56 pounds) are events for men only.

The main combined events in track and field are the decathlon for men and the pentathlon and heptathlon for women. The decathlon is a ten-event contest held over two days of competition. Many consider the Olympic decathlon champion to be the world's best all-around male athlete.

The winner of the women's five-event pentathlon at the Olympic Games is considered by many to be the world's best all-around female athlete. In 1981 the seven-event heptathlon replaced the pentathlon in track and field competition for women.

All of the events described here are outdoor contests. At indoor track and field meets, some events are not contested due to space limitations. In such cases, other events are substituted in their place.

The 35 pound weight throw is an indoor replacement for the outdoor hammer throw. The 60 yard dash and 60 yard hurdles are substitutes for the 100 yard dash and 120 yard hurdles (or their metric equivalents). Because there simply isn't enough room at indoor meets, there are no steeplechase, javelin throw or discus throw events.

Only the basic events in track and field

have been listed. There are others for men and women, boys and girls of different ages, and older athletes. They are officially regulated by The Athletics Congress of the USA.

District, regional and national championship competitions are sponsored throughout the country by The Athletics Congress. Track clubs are located in thousands of cities. Track programs are also available for young people in most public and private schools, at every age and grade level.

With television and newspaper coverage of the Olympic Games and other major track competitions, people are becoming more aware of track and field personalities and the drama of the competition itself.

There are new advances in track equipment and facilities, and training techniques and coaching. New records are set and broken every year. The track and field athlete is better today than ever before.

Track and field has a language of its own. This dictionary focuses on the current terms and definitions of this world-wide sport.

A

A.I.A.W. — Association of Intercollegiate Athletics for Women. The organization in charge of college track and field and other sports for women in the United States.

Against the clock — running against time, not against other competitors. Each athlete is timed alone and the one with the best time wins.

Age group competition — track and field contests in which young people compete against one another in groups based upon their ages.

All-around competition — a ten-event contest in which the performance of the athlete in each event is given points according to scoring tables provided by The Athletics Congress of the USA. The competitor with the highest point total for all ten events is the winner. The ten events are the 100 yard dash, 16 pound shot put, high jump, 880 yard walk, 16 pound hammer throw, pole vault, 120 yard hurdles, 56 pound weight throw, long jump and one mile run.

All-around weight competition — a five-event contest in which the best performance of the athlete in each event after three trials is given points according to official international scoring tables. The competitor with the highest point total for all five events is the winner. The five events are the 16 pound shot put, 16 pound hammer throw, discus throw, javelin throw and 35 pound weight throw.

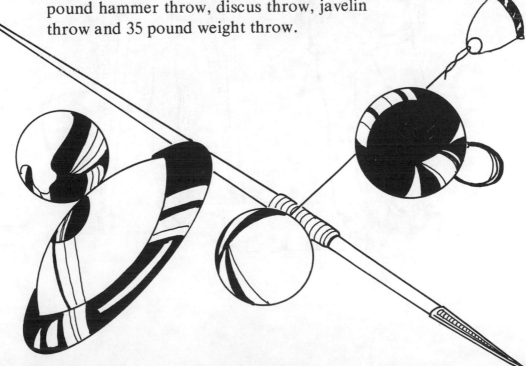

All-out — at full speed or strength; not holding anything back.

All-time — the best ever.

Alternate — someone who takes the place of another team member if he or she can't compete.

Amateur — an athlete who has never received money for taking part in sports and competes for fun.

Amateur Athletic Union — now known as The Athletics Congress of the USA. The organization in charge of track and field competition in the United States. The Congress organizes championship meets and selects teams to represent the U.S. in the Olympic Games and other world competition.

Anchor leg — the last segment of a relay race.

Anchorman — the fourth and last person to run in a relay race, usually the fastest member of the team.

19

Announcer — the track official in charge of broadcasting the results of the competition to spectators. Lets competitors know when to get ready to compete.

Approach — the run to the take-off point or movement up to the foul line by athletes in field events.

Automatic timer — an electronic device used to record the finish times of competitors.

B

Bantam — age group competition in track and field for boys and girls nine years old or under.

Baseball throw — one of the three events of the triathlon in girls' age group competition. The baseball is thrown and measured for distance like the javelin.

Baton — a hollow tube 12 inches long which is carried by runners in a relay race and handed off from one runner to another.

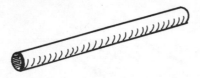

Beating the gun — moving before the starting pistol is fired. Also called "false start."

Bell lap — the last lap of a race signaled by the ringing of a bell.

Blind pass — baton exchange in sprint relay races. The outgoing runner does not look back at the incoming runner as the hand-off is being made.

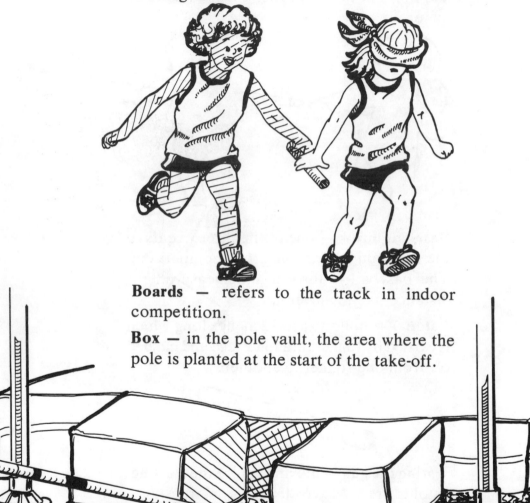

Boards — refers to the track in indoor competition.

Box — in the pole vault, the area where the pole is planted at the start of the take-off.

Boxing — when a number of runners, purposely or by chance, surround another runner to throw him off pace, keep him from moving up, or force him to go to the outside.

Break — to move off the starting line before the starting signal is given. Also called "false start."

Broad jump — see *long jump*.

Bronze medal — award given to third place finishers in a track and field event.

Bunched start — a starting position in which the runner's feet are placed close together in the starting blocks.

C

Charley horse — a muscle strain that's usually very painful and stiff.

Check mark — a mark next to the track or runway which helps an athlete measure the distance to the scratch line, or helps relay runners time a baton exchange correctly. Also called "check point."

Chop — to shorten the running stride.

Clerk of the course — the official who keeps the track meet on schedule, calls runners to the starting line and directs the drawing of lanes.

Clock — to time an athlete with a stopwatch or automatic timer.

Clocker — the person who keeps time for a race.

Close — to move up in a race or gain on the leaders.

Club — a sponsoring organization for which track and field athletes compete.

Coach — a person who teaches and trains the athletes.

Combination runner — a runner who competes in both sprints and distance events.

Combined events — the multi-events in track and field: the decathlon (ten events), the heptathlon (seven events), the pentathlon (five events), the all-around competition (ten events) and the all-around weight competition (five events).

Coubertin, Baron Pierre de — the founder of the modern Olympic movement.

Counterclockwise — the direction in which all races are run around the track. Opposite to the direction in which the hands of a clock move.

Course — the route taken by runners in a race; the running track.

Crossbar — the wood or metal bar which rests on supports across two upright bars in the high jump and pole vault. The crossbar must be cleared by the athlete without knocking it down.

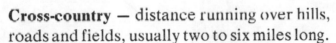

Cross-country — distance running over hills, roads and fields, usually two to six miles long.

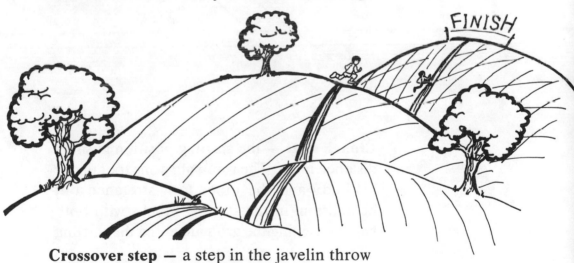

Crossover step — a step in the javelin throw in which one leg is crossed over the other just before the javelin is thrown.

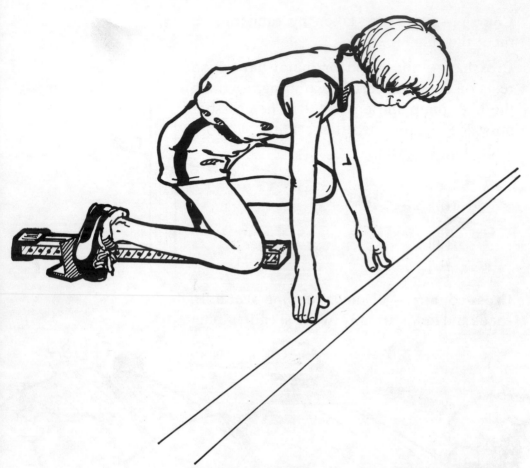

Crouch start — the starting position in short distance races. The runner has one foot under his body and the other foot stretched out behind him in the starting blocks with both hands touching the ground behind the starting line.

Cut to the pole — to move to the inside lane after a scratch start in distance races.

D

Dash — a short distance race in which contestants run at or near top speed throughout the race. Indoors there are 50, 60, 300 and 440 yard dashes. Outdoors there are 100 yard, 100 meter, 220 yard, 200 meter, 440 yard and 400 meter dashes. Also called "sprints."

Dead heat — a race in which two or more runners finish exactly even with each other.

Decathlon — a two-day contest of ten events in which the performance of the athlete in each event is given points according to a standard scoring table. The highest point total at the end of the competition wins. The first day events are the 100 meter dash, long jump, shot put, high jump and 400 meter dash. The second day events are the 110 meter hurdles, discus throw, pole vault, javelin throw and 1,500 meter run.

Dip finish — with his arms behind him, a runner pushes his shoulders forward and down into the tape at the finish of a race.

Discus — a thin, flat, circular object, used in the discus throw, made of wood or plastic with a metal rim and metal plates. It weighs about 4½ pounds for men and 2¼ pounds for women.

Discus throw — a field event in which a discus is thrown for distance from within a throwing circle.

Disqualify — to stop an athlete from competing because of bad conduct, breaking the rules, or failing to qualify.

Distance events — running races held over long distances. The two mile run, 3,000 meters, three mile run, 5,000 meters, 10,000 meters and marathon are distance events.

Distance medley — a relay race with legs of 440 yards, 880 yards, 1,320 yards and one mile, or the equivalent in meters.

Distance relay — a relay race in which each leg is run at long distances of equal length: 4 x 880 yards (two mile relay), 4 x one mile (four mile relay), or the equivalent in meters.

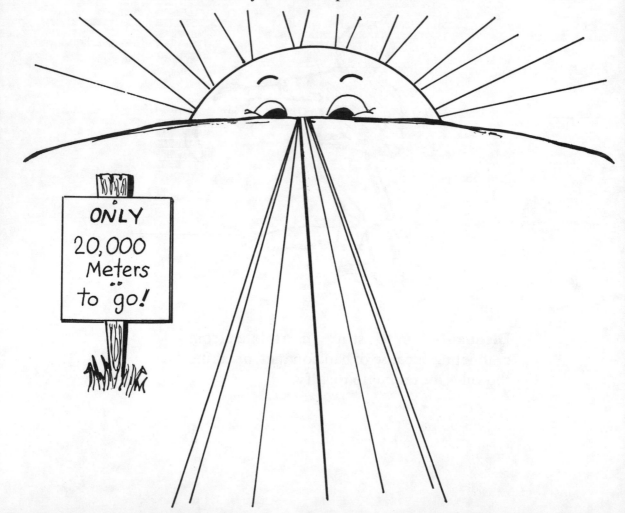

ONLY 20,000 Meters to go!

Doping — the use of drugs before or during a competition to increase strength or performance.

Drive — to run hard by pumping the arms faster through the finish.

Driving leg — the leg that gives the forward push during the take-off and running of a race.

Dual meet — a meet between two teams.

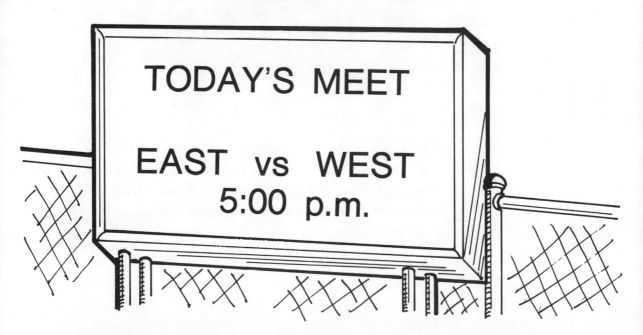

TODAY'S MEET

EAST vs WEST
5:00 p.m.

E

Elongated start — a starting position in which the starting blocks are placed many inches apart.

Event — an individual contest.

Exchange — the hand-off of the baton from one runner to the next in a relay race.

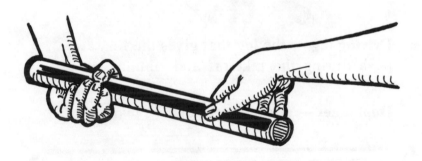

Exchange zone — a special area marked on the track, 22 yards long (10 meters), where the hand-off of the baton must take place in a relay race. Also called "passing zone" or "take-over zone."

Experimental decathlon — a special two-day, ten-event contest for women in which the performance of the athlete in each event is given points according to a standard scoring table. The highest point total at the end of the competition wins. First day events are the 100 meter dash, long jump, 8 pound 13 ounce shot put (4 kilos), high jump and 400 meter dash. Second day events are the 100 meter hurdles, discus throw, pole vault, javelin throw and 1,500 meter run. This is a test event for women, not a regular event.

F

False start — to move across the starting line with a hand or foot or out of the starting blocks before the signal is given. The competitor is disqualified on the second false start. In the combined events the competitor is disqualified on the third false start. Also called a "break."

Fartlek running — a Swedish way of training in which a runner jogs, then runs, then sprints for a distance, switching from one to the other.

Field — the area in the middle of the running track where the field events are held: the infield. Also, the total number of runners competing in a race.

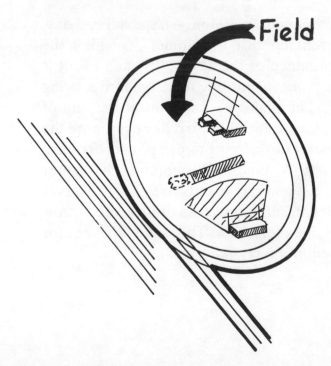

Field events — includes the high jump, pole vault, long jump, triple jump, shot put, discus throw, javelin throw, hammer throw and weight throws.

Field house — a large building used for indoor track and field competition.

Field judge — person who measures, checks and records trials in all field events.

Finish — when any part of the competitor's body (except the arms, legs or head) reaches the line at the end of the race.

Finish judges — the track officials who decide the order of finish as the runners cross the finish line.

Finish line — a line on the ground drawn across the track which marks the end of the race.

Flats — lightweight training shoes without any spikes.

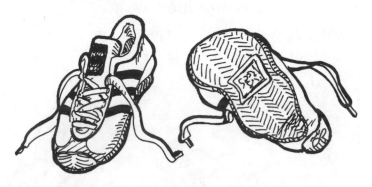

Flight — a round of trials in a field event.

Floating — running relaxed but at top speed during a race. Also called "coasting" or "gliding."

Flop — a way of high jumping in which the athlete goes over the bar head first and backward and lands on his back. Also called the "Fosbury Flop."

Foul — to break a rule as set down by The Athletics Congress of the USA which may result in the competitor's disqualification from the event. Examples include interfering with another runner, stepping over the foul line, stepping out of the lane, stepping outside the throwing circle or stepping over the take-off board. Also a trial in the field events that is not measured.

Foul line — the line in a field event which must not be stepped over to qualify for measurement in the competition.

Foul throw — in a field event, a throw counted as one trial but not measured because the competitor fouled.

Front runner — a runner who does better when he is in the lead, rather than staying back and trying to catch up. A runner who stays in the lead throughout a race.

G

Gather — to increase arm and leg action before the finish of a race.

Gold medal — award given to the first place finisher in a track and field event.

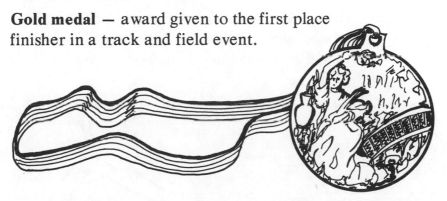

Grip — the part of the javelin, hammer or heavy weight that is held by the hand.

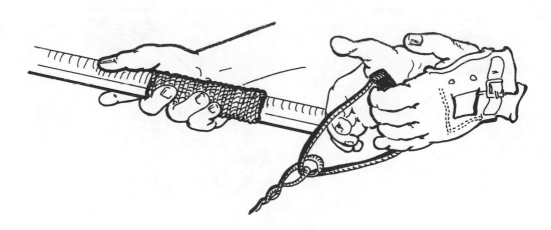

Gun lap — the last lap of a distance race signaled by the firing of a pistol.

H

Half-mile — a middle distance race of one half mile. The 880 yard run.

Hammer — a solid metal ball attached by a steel wire to a handle which weighs 16 pounds and is 4 feet long. It is used in the hammer throw.

Hammer throw — a field event in which the hammer is thrown for distance from a throwing circle.

Hamstring pull — a painful strain or pull of the tendons at the back of the leg that is common to runners.

Hand-off — the exchange of the baton in a relay race.

Hang — a way of long jumping in which the jumper brings his legs and arms back after the take-off and keeps this position until just before landing.

Harrier — a cross-country runner.

Heats — early competition to narrow the field down for the final contest.

Heavy weight — a solid metal ball attached by a steel wire to a handle grip and weighing either 35 or 56 pounds. It is used in the 35 pound weight throw and the 56 pound weight throw.

Heptathlon — a two-day seven-event contest which replaced the pentathlon for women in 1981. The performance of the athlete in each event is given points according to a standard scoring table. The highest point total at the end of the competition wins. First day events are the 100 meter hurdles, 8 pound 13 ounce shot put (4 kilos), high jump and 200 meter run; second day events are the long jump, javelin throw and 800 meter run.

High hurdles — a short race in which the runner must jump over ten 42-inch high hurdles (in high school, high hurdles are 39 inches high). Outdoor races are 120 yards and 110 meters. Indoor races are 50 yards (four hurdles), 60 yards (five hurdles) and 70 yards (six hurdles).

High jump — a field event in which each competitor tries to jump over a crossbar after a running approach. The athlete clearing the bar at its highest position is the winner. Also called the "running high jump."

Hitch kick — two strides in the air taken by a long jumper after the take-off to keep his balance and body control during the jump.

Hop step — a step in the javelin throw. The thrower takes a low hop on one foot and steps forward with the other as the javelin is thrown.

Hop, step, and jump — see *triple jump*.

Hundred — a dash run over a distance of 100 yards or 100 meters.

Hurdle — a wood and metal barrier which the runner must jump over in the hurdles races or the steeplechase. The hurdle is 36 to 42 inches high for men, and 30 to 33 inches high for women, depending on the length of the race. In the steeplechase, hurdles are long beams, three feet high, that are attached to the track and can be stepped on or jumped over by the runner.

Hurdles race — a race run over hurdles from 50 yards long, for boys and girls in age group competition, to 400 meters or 440 yards long for men and women.

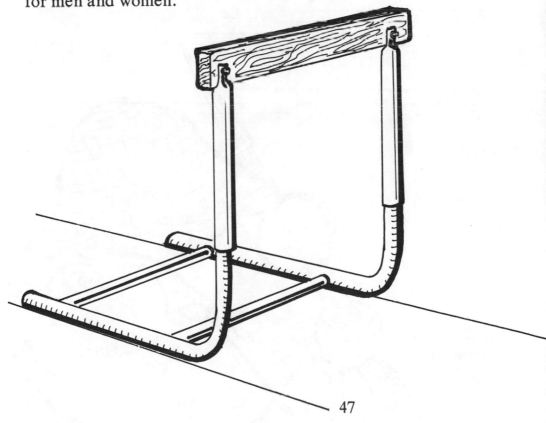

I

Indoor events — events contested within an enclosed area or building.

Inside — the lane nearest the field area or pole.

Inspector — official who assists the referee in watching for fouls and makes sure the rules are followed during the competition.

Inspector of implements — track official who weighs and measures all track and field equipment used in competition.

Interference — the stopping of another runner's freedom of movement during a race by bumping or touching. Usually results in being disqualified.

Intermediate — age group competition in track and field for boys and girls 14 and 15 years old.

Intermediate hurdles — a hurdles race of 440 yards or 400 meters with ten 36-inch high hurdles for men (30 inches high for women) set at distances around the track. In high school the race is 330 yards with eight hurdles.

International Amateur Athletic Federation — organization in charge of international track and field competition. Makes decisions on all world records.

Interval training — a series of runs at different distances which is broken up by periods of jogging or walking.

Invitational — a track and field meet open only to those invited.

Isometric weight training — method of training that develops muscles by pushing against a solid object that can't move.

Isotonic weight training — method of training that develops muscles by pushing against an object that moves.

J

Javelin — a long metal or wood spear attached to a sharp pointed metal tip. The men's javelin weighs about 1 pound 12 ounces and is about 8 feet 6 inches to just under 9 feet long; the women's javelin weighs about 1 pound 5 ounces and is no longer than 7 feet 6½ inches. The cord hand grip is placed at the center balance point.

Javelin throw — a field event in which the javelin is thrown for distance with one hand from a running approach.

Jog — to run at a steady but relaxed pace as a conditioning or warm-up exercise.

Judges of race walking — the track officials who watch the competitors to see if they are competing according to the rules of race walking. They may warn or disqualify an athlete.

Jumping events — field events in which competitors must jump or vault for height or distance. The high jump, long jump, triple jump and pole vault are all jumping events.

Jump-off — a jumping contest used to determine the first place winner when there is a tie between competitors in the high jump or pole vault.

Jump the gun — to start a race before the starting signal is given. See also *false start*.

Junior — track and field competition for girls 14 to 18 years old and boys 19 years old and under.

K

Kick — a sudden burst of speed near the end of a race.

L

Landing — the position of the feet and body at the end of a vault or jump in field events. Also, the first step down after clearing a hurdle in a hurdles race.

Landing beds — an area of sawdust, shavings or foam rubber on which pole vaulters and jumpers land after vaulting or jumping. Also called "landing pit."

Lanes — separate side by side running areas on the track, each about four feet wide, in which competitors must run for either part of a race or for the whole race. Lanes are assigned by draw or by time recorded in trial heats. A standard running track has eight lanes.

Lap — one time around the track. Also, to build up a lead over another runner by one full run around the track.

Lap scorer — a track official who keeps records of the laps run by each competitor in races of 1,500 meters or longer. The lap scorer tells each athlete how many more laps have to be run and rings bell on the final lap.

Layout — the part of the high jump in which the jumper goes over the crossbar with his body parallel to the bar.

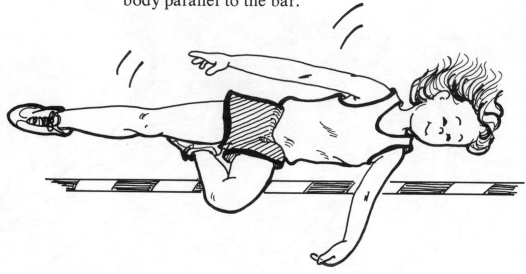

Lead — to be in front or in first place.

Lead arm — the arm opposite the lead leg.

Lead leg — the leg that goes first in hurdling or running events. The first leg of a relay race.

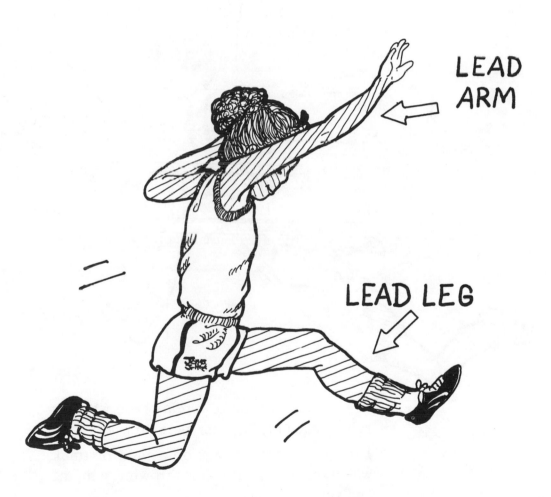

LEAD ARM

LEAD LEG

Lead-off — to run the first leg or section of a relay race.

Leaning into the tape — bending a shoulder into the finish tape at the last second to win a close race.

Leg — that section of a relay race which is run by each of the team members.

Line — white markings on a field or track which show the limits of the throwing, jumping and running areas.

Long jump — a field event in which a competitor jumps for distance from a running start. Also called "broad jump" or "running long jump."

Low hurdles — a hurdles race of 180 yards, run over eight hurdles, or 220 yards or 200 meters, run over ten hurdles. The hurdles are set at distances around the track and each hurdle is 30 inches high.

M

Marathon — a race run over a course of 26 miles, 385 yards.

Mark — a competitor's position at the starting line. Also, the point where a long jumper or triple jumper lands, or where an object in the throwing events touches down first.

TRACK AND FIELD AREA

Competitors and Officials ONLY!!

Marshal — the track official in charge of security. Lets only competitors and other officials in the track and field area.

Masters — men over 40 years old and women over 30 years old who compete in special track and field events, long distance running and race walking competition.

Match race — a race between two people.

Medium start — a starting position in which the starting blocks are placed one behind the other.

Medley relay — a relay race in which each leg is a different distance.

Meet — a track competition for individuals or clubs.

Metric — a system of measurement using the meter and the gram: one meter equals 39.37 inches and one gram equals .0022046 pounds. The metric system is used in the Olympic Games and by most countries of the world for track and field measurement.

Metric mile — the 1,500 meter run. It is the metric race closest to the mile run (.93 miles).

A GRAM OF PREVENTION IS WORTH A KILOGRAM OF CURE.

Middle distance race — usually the 800 meters, the half mile or 880 yard run, and the mile run or 1,500 meters. Some people feel that the mile run and 1,500 meters are long distance races.

Midget — age group competition in track and field for boys and girls ten and 11 years old.

Mile relay — a relay race in which each leg is a quarter of a mile long (440 yards).

Mile run — a race one mile long (four laps around a standard quarter mile track).

Move — getting into position to gain on or overtake the leader of a race.

Multiple meet — a track meet with more than four teams competing.

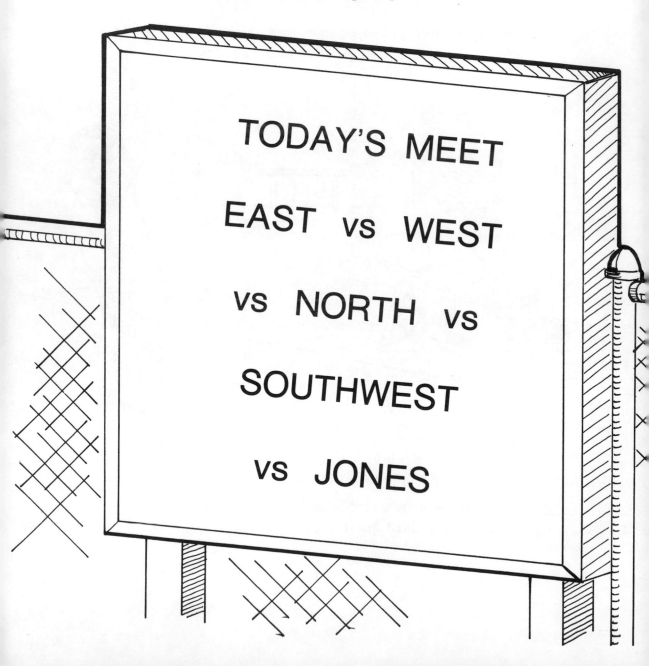

TODAY'S MEET

EAST vs WEST

vs NORTH vs

SOUTHWEST

vs JONES

N

NCAA — National Collegiate Athletic Association. The organization in charge of college track and field and other sports for men in the United States.

Novice — an athlete who has not won an individual first, second or third place award in any competition of running, race walking or field events.

O

Official — the person in charge of seeing that the rules and regulations in track and field are carried out: a referee or judge.

Off season — the time of year when there are no track and field competitions — usually during the fall and winter months. (Many athletes train regularly throughout the year anyway.)

Olympic Games — international amateur sports competition held every four years in different countries throughout the world. Athletes from more than 120 nations compete against each other in over 22 different sports.

On your marks — the starter's command to the runners to get into their starting positions behind the starting line.

Open meet — a track meet open to anyone who wants to compete.

Outclass — to easily beat the other competitors in a race or field event.

Outdistance — to beat the other competitors by a large amount.

Outkick — to have a stronger burst of speed at the finish of a race than the other runners.

Outrun — to run faster than another competitor.

Outside — the lane farthest from the field area.

Overdistance — a way of training in which a runner increases his stamina by running distances longer than his regular event.

Overtrain — to train too hard for a meet and peak too soon so that the performance of the athlete is not his or her best effort.

P

Pace — the speed at which a race is run. Also, to save energy for later in the race.

Pack — a group of runners bunched up in a race.

Pan-American Games — an international amateur sports competition held every four years between Olympic Games. North, Central and South American countries take part and more than 19 sports are contested.

Pass — the baton hand-off from one runner to another in a relay race. Another word for "exchange." Also, to decide to wait for a greater height instead of trying to vault or jump over a height in the pole vault or high jump.

Passer — the runner who hands off the baton during the exchange in a relay race.

Peak — the high point of training and conditioning when the athlete's performance is best.

Pentathlon — a one or two day, five-event contest for women, which includes the 100 meter hurdles, 8 pound 13 ounce (4 kilo) shot put, high jump, long jump and 800 meter run. The performance of the athlete in each event is given points according to a standard scoring table, and the competitor with the most points wins. The men's pentathlon is a one day, five-event contest which includes the long jump, javelin throw, 200 meters, discus throw and 1,500 meter run. Scoring is the same as the men's decathlon.

Photo finish — a race too close to call the order of finish without looking at the photograph. To use a photographic device to record the finish of a race.

Photo finish panel — a group of judges who examine the photographs taken of a race to decide the winner.

Pit — the landing area for jumping events built to cushion the force of landing with foam rubber or other soft material.

Plant — to thrust the pole in the take-off box just before leaving the ground in the pole vault.

Pocket — a position in which a runner is closed in by other competitors in a race and can't move around them. The runner is hemmed in.

Points — scoring units in track and field which decide team standings and the order of finish of the pentathlon, decathlon and other combined events.

Pole — a long, flexible pole usually made of fiberglass and used by vaulters to swing up and over the crossbar in the pole vault. The bending action of the pole throws the vaulters high in the air.

Pole lane — the lane closest to the infield area of the track: lane one.

Pole vault — a field event in which each competitor uses a long pole to vault over a crossbar after a running approach. The athlete clearing the bar at the highest level is the winner.

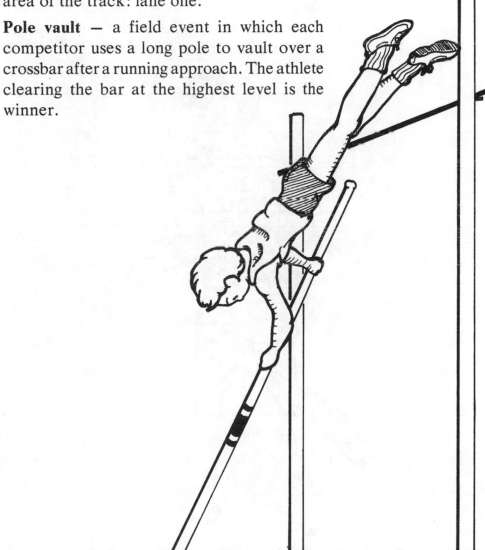

Preliminary — early competition to narrow the field down for the final contests.

Press steward — a track official who keeps the press informed of the names of competitors and their recorded times or distances in the events.

Professional — an athlete who receives money for taking part in sports, advertising a product or promoting sports equipment.

Putting the shot — using the entire body to thrust the shot outward from the shoulder with the arm guiding in the effort.

Q

Quadrangular meet — a track meet in which four teams compete against each other.

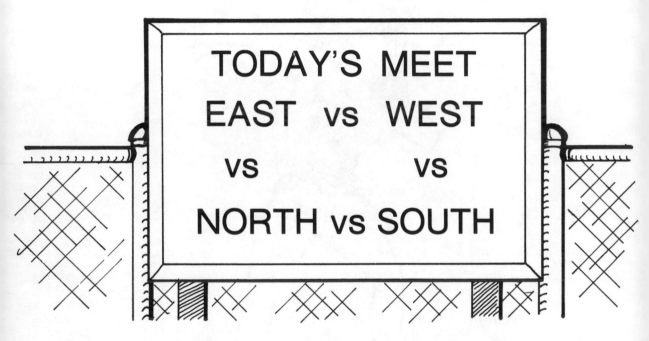

TODAY'S MEET
EAST vs WEST
vs   vs
NORTH vs SOUTH

Qualifying round — early competition which determines which athletes will compete in the actual event.

Quarterfinals — the race or round before the semifinal competition.

Quarter mile — a race run over a distance of one fourth of a mile. The 440 yard dash.

78

R

Rabbit — a runner who sets a fast pace in a race.

Race walking — a walking race in which there is always constant contact with the ground by one foot of the competitor. During each step, the leg must be straightened for one second.

Recall — when the starter calls back the competitors after a false start and another starting signal is given.

Receiver — the runner who gets the baton during a hand-off in a relay race.

Record — the official best performance in an event.

Referee — the track official at all meets who makes sure that the rules of The Athletics Congress are carried out and decides all questions during the competition.

Regional championships — track and field competitions conducted every year in 14 different areas of the country by The Athletics Congress.

Relay race — a race in which teams of four runners compete against each other. Each runner covers the same distance or one leg of the race at a time. A baton is passed from one runner to another in all legs of the race. Standard relays are the 400 meters (4 x 100), 440 yards (4 x 110), 1,600 meters (4 x 400), mile relay (4 x 440 yards) and the two mile relay (4 x 880 yards).

Resin — a substance used on the hands of competitors in the throwing events and pole vault to give them a better grip.

Reverse — to change the position of the feet after the toss in a throwing event.

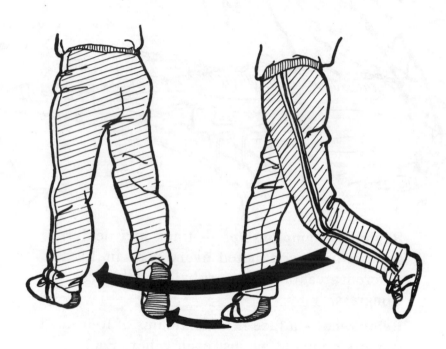

Rolling start — an illegal start in which the runner moves from the set position just before the starting signal is given.

Run — a race of more than 440 yards or 400 meters. Also, a running approach by a competitor to gain speed before jumping or throwing.

Runaway — an easy win.

Running events — foot races in which competitors run short, middle and long distances, jump over hurdles and other barriers and take part in team relays, usually around an oval-shaped track.

Runway — an approach area for running up to the take-off point in the pole vault, high jump, long jump, triple jump and javelin throw.

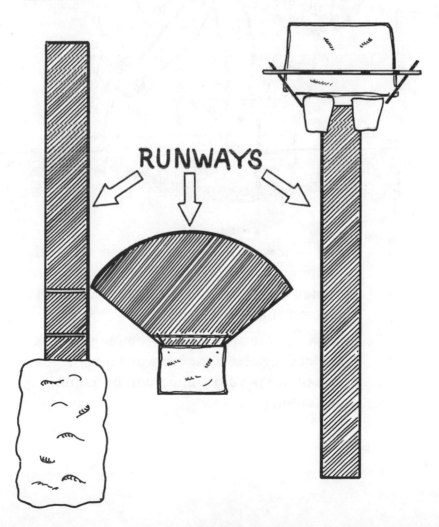

RUNWAYS

S

Sail — a way of long jumping in which the jumper gets into the landing position immediately after the take-off. It is recommended for beginners.

Scissors — a way of high jumping in which the lead leg clears the bar while the jumper is in a sitting position, and then the trailing leg clears the bar.

Scorer — the track official in charge of collecting and recording times, heights, distances, order of finish and team point totals in a meet.

Scratch — to foul a field event or to be cut from competition.

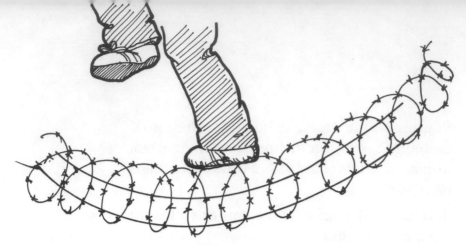

Scratch line — a line in the field events over which a competitor must not step or it will be counted as a foul.

Scratch start — a start in which the runners line up straight across the track and are allowed to move inside after the first turn.

Season — the time of year when there is track and field competition — usually during the spring and summer months.

Sector — in throwing events, the area stretching out from the throwing circle where all throws must fall to be counted as legal throws.

Sector flags — banners which mark the outer edge of the sector in which all throws must fall to be counted.

Semifinals — the next-to-last race or round before the final competition.

Senior — the highest level of competition. It is open to all male athletes and young women age 14 and older.

Set — the command by the starter after "on your marks" when competitors are in the starting position waiting for the starting signal. In dashes, runners are usually in a crouch with hips raised, hands on the ground and the body leaning forward but not moving.

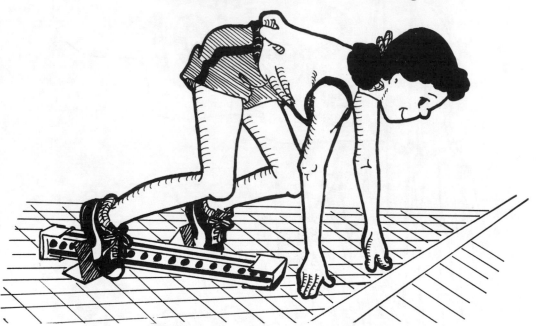

Set-up — to force another runner into a position where he can be easily passed in a race.

Shin splints — common injury to runners in which there is intense pain and swelling in the shin. The shin is the front part of the leg between the knee and the ankle.

Shot — a smooth metal ball that is used in the shot put. It weighs 16 pounds for men and 8 pounds 13 ounces for women (4 kilos). High school boys use a 12 pound shot.

Shot put — a field event in which a shot is thrown for distance from a throwing circle with a thrusting motion using one arm at shoulder level.

Shuffle — to move one foot in one direction and bring the other foot up to the same place while moving sideways or forward.

Shuffle step — to run fast without lifting the knees high.

Shuttle relay — a relay race which is run back and forth in two directions with or without hurdles. The first and third runners line up to run in one direction and the second and fourth line up on the opposite side of the track to run in the other direction.

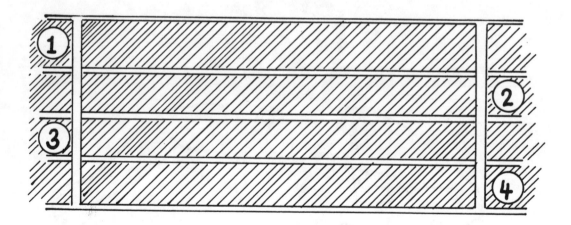

Silver medal — award given to second place finishers in a track and field event.

Sitting on the hurdle — an improper way of hurdling in which the hurdler is in an upright position when he goes over the hurdles.

Skimming the hurdle — an improper way of hurdling in which the front leg of the hurdler barely clears the top of the hurdle.

Speed work — sprints run in training so runners can develop a kick or a faster pace for passing.

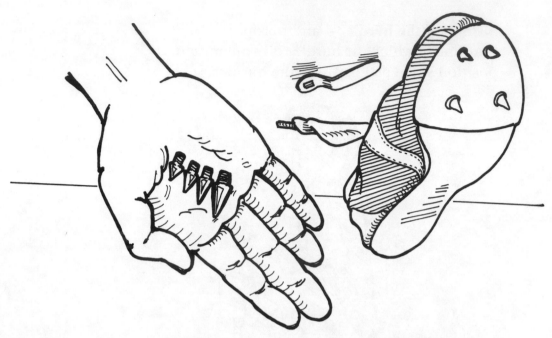

Spikes — a pair of track shoes with sharp nail-like points that stick out from the sole up to one inch long. They are used to get a firm grip on the ground during competition.

Splits — the measured times for a runner at certain points in a distance race (every quarter mile, half mile or mile).

Sportsmanship — being courteous and friendly when winning or losing, taking no unfair advantages over the other competitors: the expected behavior of an athlete.

Sprint — to go at top speed. Also, a short race up to 400 meters (or 440 yards) run at full speed. Another word for "dash."

Sprint medley — a relay race in which each leg is run at sprint distances of different lengths: 440, 220, 220, 880 yards (or the equivalent in meters).

Sprint pass — a baton exchange in a sprint relay or sprint medley in which the outgoing runner does not look back at the incoming runner as the hand-off is being made.

Sprint relay — a relay race in which each leg is run at sprint distances of equal length: 4 x 110 (440 yards), 4 x 220 (880 yards) or the equivalent in meters.

Sprint start — a starting position in sprint races in which the runner crouches with both feet in the starting blocks. When the starting signal is given, the runner pushes off against the blocks for a fast start. Also called "crouch start."

Staggered start — used in races in which the runners must stay in their lanes around one or more turns. The starting line for each lane is further ahead of the other as the lanes advance from the inside to the outside of the track. Though the runners on the outside seem to have a head start, the distances for all competitors are equal since the outside runners have a greater distance to cover around the turn.

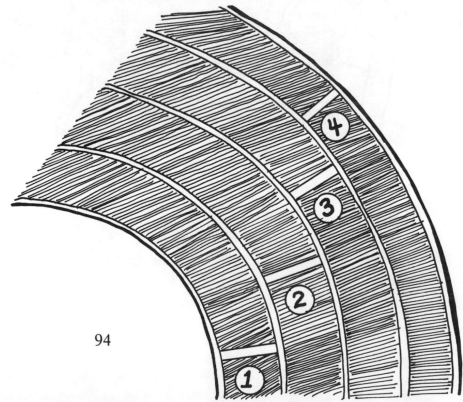

Stamina — the staying power and endurance to finish a long distance competition.

Standing broad jump — a field event in which each competitor jumps for distance from a standing position without a running start. Also called "standing long jump."

Standing high jump — a field event in which each competitor jumps for height from a standing position without a running start.

Standing long jump — see *standing broad jump.*

Standing start — the start of a race in which competitors are standing and not crouching in the starting blocks.

Starter — the track official who fires the pistol to start a race, decides false starts and signals the bell or gun lap.

Starter's pistol — a pistol which fires blanks and is used to signal the start of a race and the start of the gun lap.

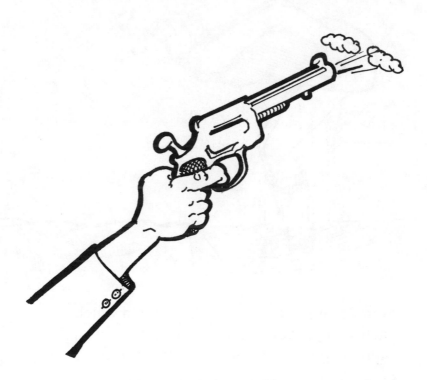

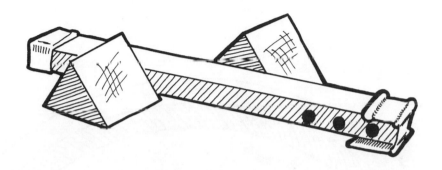

Starting blocks — two adjustable blocks secured to the track in which runners fit their feet and push off for a fast start. They are used in short races not more than 440 yards or 400 meters in length.

Starting line — a line marked on the track which competitors must stay behind until the starting signal is given.

Steeplechase — a 3,000 meter (1.9 mile) race in which competitors must jump over 28 hurdles and seven water jumps spread over the course. Athletes may hurdle over, or jump onto and then over, the 3 feet high, 5 inch thick, 13 feet wide hurdles.

Steroids — illegal drugs used by some athletes to build up their muscles quickly so that they can perform better.

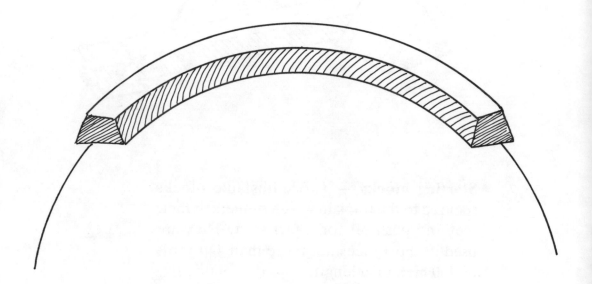

Stopboard — a curved block of wood or metal fixed to the ground at the front edge of the shot put throwing circle which keeps competitors from stepping out of the circle. Also called "toeboard." In the pole vault, the stopboard catches the pole after the vaulter lets go of it at the beginning of a vault.

Straddle — a way of high jumping in which the jumper crosses over the bar parallel to it on his stomach and then brings his trailing leg over the bar.

Straightaway — the straight part of the track between turns.

Sub-masters — athletes 30 to 34 and 35 to 39 years of age who compete in special track and field events, long distance running and race walking competition.

Surveyor — the track official in charge of inspecting and measuring the track and runways, throwing circles, sectors and other areas in the field events.

Swedish relay — a sprint medley with legs of 100, 200, 300 and 400 meters (or the equivalent in yards) in outdoor competition, and 400, 200, 200 and 300 meters (or the equivalent in yards) in indoor competition.

Sweep — winning all the events or all the places in a competition.

Swifter, higher, stronger — the motto of the Olympic Games.

T

Take-off — the point at which the athlete leaves the ground to jump or vault for height or distance.

Take-off board — a flat piece of wood, level with the runway at the end of the long jump and triple jump, which helps the jumper in his take-off. The far edge of the board is the scratch line and if any part of the athlete's foot touches beyond the line or off the board on either side, it is a foul.

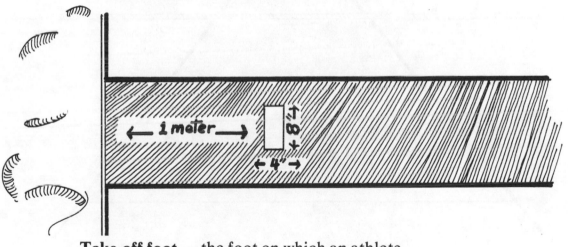

Take-off foot — the foot on which an athlete begins his take-off. The take-off foot helps push the body up and off the ground.

Take-off leg — the leg that gives the push when an athlete jumps for distance or height, or clears a hurdle.

Take-over zone — the area in relay races in which each runner must pass the baton to the next runner. Also called "exchange zone" or "passing zone."

Tape — a string or thread which is tied four feet above and directly over the finish line across the track and easily broken by the runners as they cross the finish line.

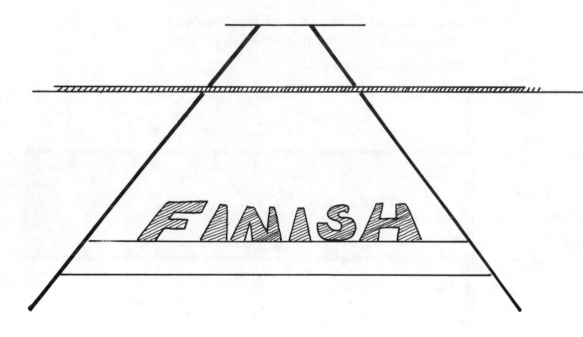

Tartan — the trade name for the artificial surface used on running tracks in place of dirt or cinder.

Team trophy — an award given to the team scoring the most points in a championship competition.

Tendonitis — pain and swelling of the tendon in the elbow, shoulder or knee.

The Athletics Congress of the United States of America — the organization in charge of track and field competition in the United States. The Congress sets down rules for all events and selects teams that represent the United States in the Olympic Games and other world competitions. It was formerly known as the Amateur Athletic Union.

Throwing cage — in the hammer and discus throw, a 16 foot high fenced-in area, open only at the end where the throw is made. The area is enclosed on three sides to keep the spectators safe.

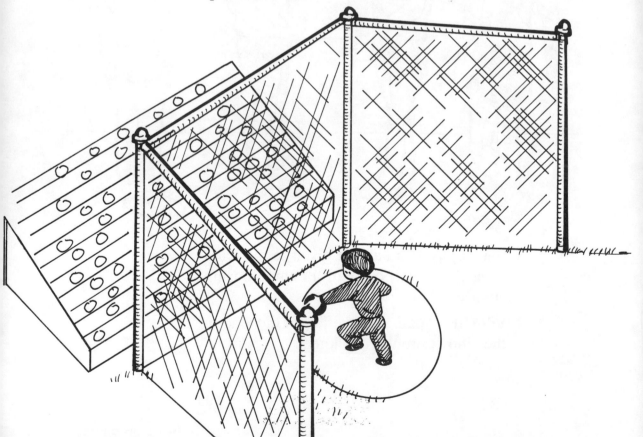

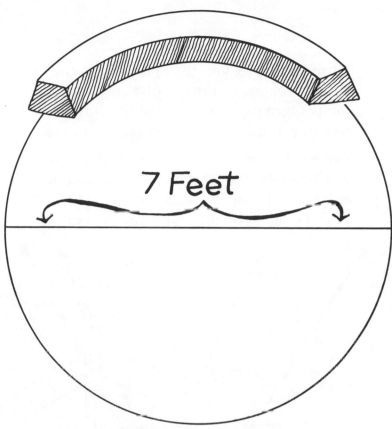

7 Feet

Throwing circle — in the shot put, weight throws, discus throw and hammer throw, the circular area in which a competitor must stay in order to have the throw qualify for measurement. The throwing circle is seven feet across, except in the discus throw where it is 8 feet 2½ inches across.

Throwing events — field events in which competitors throw, hurl or put an object for distance. The shot put, javelin, discus, hammer, heavy weights and baseball throw are all throwing events.

Throwing line — the curved line at the end of the approach in the javelin throw. The competitor must not step over this line while making a throw or it will be counted as a foul.

Throwing sector — the area in throwing events in which the shot, javelin, discus, hammer, weights and baseball must land in order to have the throw qualify for measurement.

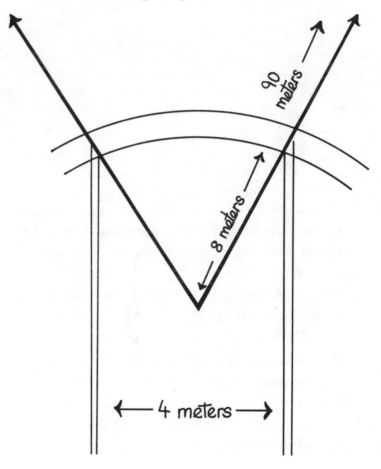

90 meters

8 meters

←— 4 meters —→

Tie — when two or more competitors have the same score, time, height or distance in a track and field event. In running events, ties for first place may stand or competitors may compete again. In throwing events, ties for first place are broken by the next best throw. In jumping events, ties are broken by the next best jump, fewest attempts at the winning height, lowest number of misses or a jump-off if nothing else works.

Tied up — muscle fatigue because of over-straining. Also, to be unable to relax due to tension and nervousness.

Time — the hours, minutes, seconds, tenths or hundredths of seconds it takes for an athlete to compete in an event. Competitors are timed separately and not against each other, with each trying to have the best time. Also called "against time" or "against the clock."

Timekeeper — a track official who reads and records the times of competitors from the automatic timer.

Timer — a track official who is in charge of timing the runner in competition. Times are recorded by using stopwatches or automatic devices.

Time trial — a practice race to measure the speed of the athlete and his physical conditioning.

Toeboard — a stopboard used in the shot put. See also *stopboard*.

Torso — the trunk of the body which must cross the finish line. It does not include the head, neck, arms, hands, legs or feet.

Track — an oval course for running, usually one quarter mile or 400 meters around, with two wide turns and six to eight running lanes. An indoor track is smaller and about one-tenth of a mile around.

Track and field — competition in running, jumping, throwing and walking events on a running track and the enclosed infield.

Trackside — next to or close to the track.

Tracksuit — a sweatsuit.

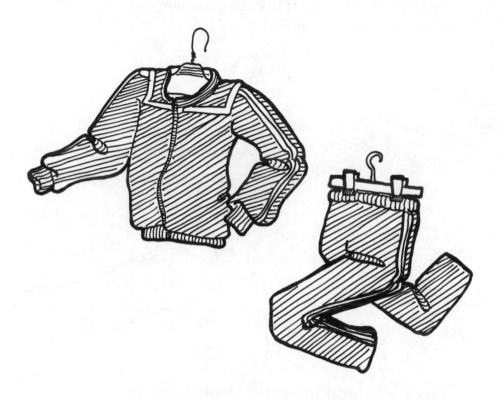

Trailing leg — the leg that gives the push for the take-off when an athlete jumps for distance or height and follows behind the body during the first part of the jump. Also, the back leg in hurdling. Another word for "take-off leg."

Training — exercises to increase strength, stamina, endurance and skills in a sport. Also includes a well-balanced diet and good sleeping habits.

Trial — an attempt in a field event. Each competitor is given three preliminary trials and those with the best performances go on to the final which consists of three more trials. The best performance in any of the trials, preliminary or final, will count in the results of the contest. In the high jump and pole vault, an athlete is eliminated from competition if he misses three trials in a row.

Transition — driving up and out of the starting blocks into a smooth running stride.

Trial heats — early competition to narrow down the field for the final contest. See *heats*.

Triangular meet — a meet in which three teams compete against each other.

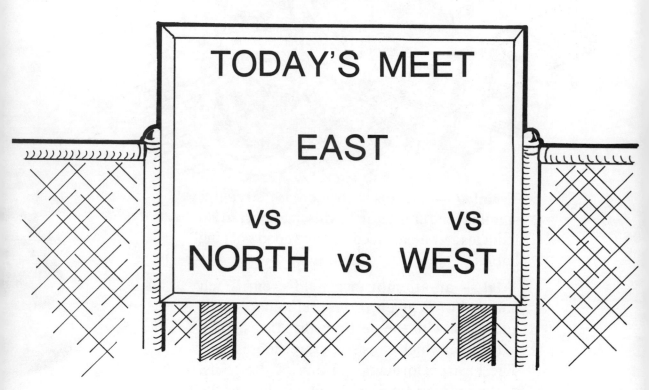

Triathlon — a three-event contest for boys and girls age group competition which consists of the 100 meter dash, the high jump, and the baseball throw for girls or the 6 pound shot put for boys.

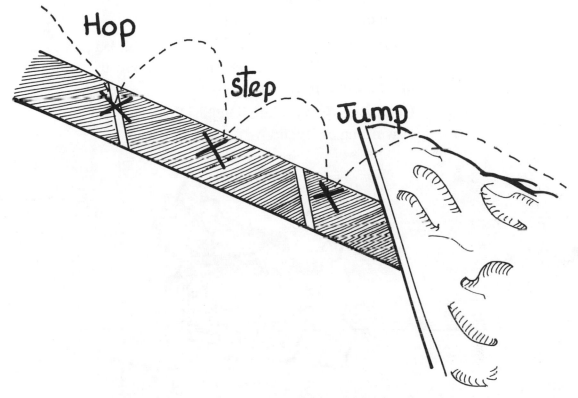

Triple jump — a field event in which each competitor hops and lands on the take-off foot, steps and lands on the other foot, and jumps landing on both feet for distance from a running start. Also called "hop, step, and jump."

Turn — the curved part of the running track as it changes direction.

U

Unattached — not competing with a team or club; competing as an individual.

Underdistance — a way of training in which a runner runs distances less than his event to increase his speed.

Underdog — an athlete who has little chance of winning an event.

United States Olympic Committee — committee that selects and prepares U.S. men's and women's teams for the Olympic Games and Pan American Games. Also develops national training centers and is the U.S. representative to the International Olympic Committee.

Unlap — to make up a lap after being lapped by an opponent.

Unsportsmanlike conduct — bad behavior of an athlete for which he may be disqualified, including bothering an opponent, fighting, hitting an official, bad language, etc.

Up — ready and prepared, looking forward to a competition.

Upright — the two posts which support the crossbars in the high jump and pole vault.

Upset — to beat the favorite in a competition.

V

Vault — to attempt a jump over the crossbar in the pole vault.

Vaulting box — in the pole vault, the area in which the pole is planted at the beginning of a vault. Also called a "take-off box."

Victory lap — an extra lap run by the winner at the end of a race.

Visual pass — a baton exchange in distance relay races in which the outgoing runner watches the incoming runner as the hand-off is being made.

W

Warm-down — light exercises after competition or heavy workouts to allow an athlete to relax and get back to normal.

Warm-up — exercises to loosen and stretch the muscles and increase blood circulation before a competition or heavy workout.

Water jump — a pool of water in the steeple-chase event with a three foot high hurdle at the front. The pool slopes up from a depth of 2 feet 4 inches at the hurdle end to the level of the field at the far end. The competitor can jump over or through the water by jumping or stepping on the hurdle.

Weights — the shot put, hammer, 35 pound weight and 56 pound weight, which are thrown for distance in field events. See also *heavy weights*.

Weight throw — field events in which a 35 pound or 56 pound weight is thrown for distance from within a throwing circle. The 35 pound weight throw replaces the hammer throw at indoor meets.

Weight training — a way of training in which an athlete slowly lifts more and more weights to develop strength and stamina, paying special attention to the muscles used in his event.

118

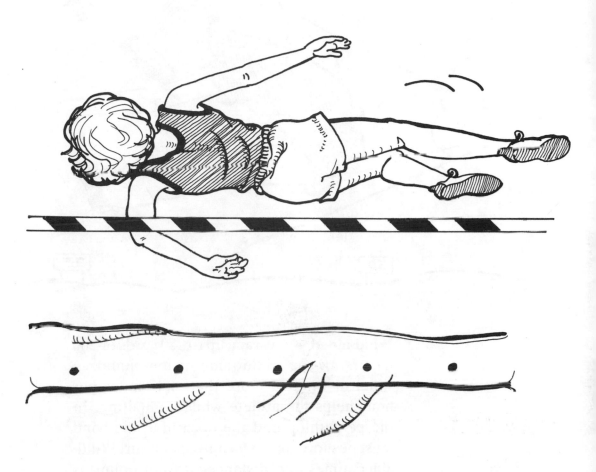

Western roll — a way of high jumping in which the jumper goes over the bar on his side with both legs together.

Win — to gain a victory; to finish in first place.

Wind — to breathe normally during heavy exercise or competition.

Wind-aided — any race up to 220 yards or 200 meters, or the triple jump or long jump, in which a wind of more than 4.47 miles per hour helps the athlete while competing. In the pentathlon and the decathlon the wind must be more than 8.94 miles per hour. Wind-aided times and distances do not count as official track and field records.

Wind gauge operator — a track official in charge of measuring the direction and wind velocity for all running events up to 220 yards or 200 meters, the long jump, the triple jump and certain events in the pentathlon and the decathlon.

Wind sprints — short sprints run in training to build up an athlete's wind and stamina.

Wire to wire — from start to finish.

Workout — exercises to keep in shape or to practice athletic skills.

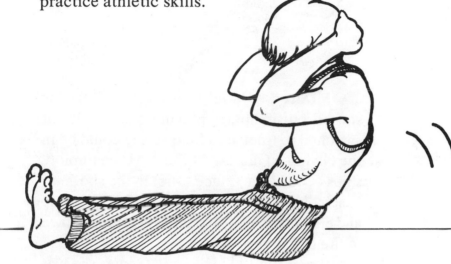

World-class — the highest quality in the world.

World record — the top performance in the world.

Y

Young men — age group competition in track and field for boys 16 and 17 years of age.

Youth — age group competition in track and field for boys and girls 12 and 13 years of age.

Mildred "Babe" Didrikson Zaharias started out in sports playing basketball but switched to track and field so she could be in the Olympic Games. At the AAU championships of 1932, she placed first in the shot put, baseball throw, javelin throw, broad jump and 80 meter hurdles. She tried for first place in the high jump.

But at the 1932 Olympic Games she was allowed to enter only three events. She set world records in the javelin throw and the 80 meter hurdles. Because of a technicality she placed second in the high jump.

After the Olympic Games, Babe broke or equaled every women's Olympic track-and-field record, but the AAU ruled that she lose her amateur status when her picture appeared for a car advertisement.

She played professional golf, won over a million dollars and in 1950 was voted the greatest woman athlete of the half century.

One of the greatest track-and-field athletes ever was Jesse Owens, called "The Tan Cyclone." On May 25, 1935, in less than one hour, Owens broke three world records (long jump, 220 yard dash, 220 yard low hurdles) and tied another (100 yard dash).

Adolf Hitler, the Nazi dictator, believed that Jews and blacks were weak and inferior, and that German athletes were the best in the world. Jesse Owens, who was black, proved him wrong at the 1936 Olympic Games in Berlin. He won four gold medals, including the 100 meter dash, the 200 meter dash and long jump. He was also a member of the winning U.S. 400 meter relay team.

Reporters called Fanny Blankers-Koen the "Flying Housewife" and the "Marvelous Mamma." She married her track coach and had two sons.

In 1948 Fanny set four world records for women — the high jump (5 feet 7¼ inches), broad jump (20 feet 6 inches), 100 meter dash (11.0 seconds) and 100 yard dash (10.8 seconds).

At 30 Fanny was the oldest female athlete at the Olympic Games in London. Many said she was too old to compete. Fanny had the last laugh. She became the first woman in Olympic history to win three individual track and field gold medals, as well as a gold medal in the 400 meter relay. She won the 100 meter dash, 80 meter hurdles and 200 meter dash. Holland has won only four gold medals in running at the Olympics and Fanny Blankers-Koen won them all.

Jim Thorpe, a Sac-and-Fox Indian, may be the greatest all-around athlete of all time. While at Carlisle Indian School in Pennsylvania he competed in track, football, baseball, basketball, tennis, lacrosse, swimming and gymnastics. One summer he even played semi-professional baseball.

At the 1912 Olympics in Sweden, Thorpe won both the ten-event decathlon and the five-event pentathlon, the only man ever to have done so.

In 1913, the AAU decided that Thorpe was not an amateur since he had been paid for playing baseball. He returned his awards and his name was taken off the record books. Thorpe went on to play professional baseball and football, but will always be remembered for his track-and-field achievements.

ABOUT THE AUTHOR

PHYLLIS RAYBIN EMERT has been a freelance writer since 1975 and a sports enthusiast for much longer. Born in Philadelphia, she earned a Bachelor's Degree at the State University of New York at Stony Brook and a Master's Degree at Penn. State. She now lives in southern California with her husband and young son and daughter.

Ms. Emert has written extensively on sports for magazines for five years. She is a dedicated scrabble player, jogger and bicyclist, as well as an avid reader and baseball fan.

ABOUT THE ILLUSTRATOR

MARIETTA FOSTER SMITH has a studio in Greensboro, North Carolina, where she illustrates books and stories, does watercolors, oil portraits and fabric design. She is married and the mother of four children who frequently model for her illustrations. A graduate of the University of North Carolina at Greensboro, she is a jogger and is active in community affairs.